# TABLE OF CONTENTS

Introduction

Different Types of Vegan Diets

Vegan Diets and Heart Health

Foods to Avoid

Supplements to Consider

A Vegan Sample Menu for One Week

How to Eat Vegan at Restaurants

Supplements You Need on a Vegan Diet

Thug Kicthen Vegan diet recipes

BBQ CHICKPEA COLLARD WRAPS

Roasted Cauliflower & Brussels Sprouts

Slow Cooker Mashed Potatoes & Cranberry Mushroom Sauce

Roasted Broccolini with Mushrooms in Balsamic Sauce

VEGAN WINTER SALAD

KALE AND CAULIFLOWER SOUP

COCONUT CURRY SOUP W/ SWEET POTATO NOODLES

ONE-POT RED LENTIL AND BUTTERNUT SQUASH CHILI

FRENCH LENTIL & CHICKPEA SOUP (VEGAN)

VEGAN CLASSIC LEEK AND POTATO SOUP

Easy Spicy Vegetable Soup

Warm Quinoa and Roasted Vegetable Salad

Carrot, Red Lentil, & Spinach Soup

ROASTED BUTTERNUT SQUASH, KALE AND CRANBERRY COUSCOUS

CREAMY VEGAN BUTTERNUT SQUASH SOUP WITH ROASTED VEGETABLES

Conclusion

# INTRODUCTION

Thug Kitchen, a three-year-old vegan blog that seasons its recipes with profanities, readers are exhorted to eat their [expletive] vegetables and be badasses in the kitchen. It's a mischievous manifesto for inexpensive, healthy eating, leavened with the sort of humor that fueled the bedtime parody "Go the [expletive] to Sleep." "Eat a [expletive] salad. It's like plant nachos," is a typical entry.

The creators of "TK" (as they call it for short) are Matt Holloway and Michelle Davis, now both 30, and both vegans. They began it, when he was working as a production assistant in a film company and she was a team member at Whole Foods, as a semiserious project: some health tips wrapped up in some jokes and a lot of cursing.

The aftermath was profound: The Tumblr blog had so many hits, its Google Analytics crashed. Saveur magazine gave Thug Kitchen its award for the best new food blog. It accrued millions of loyal readers, and a book deal from Rodale.

Veganism is defined as a way of living that attempts to exclude all forms of animal exploitation and cruelty, whether for food, clothing or any other purpose.

For these reasons, the vegan diet is devoid of all animal products, including meat, eggs and dairy.

# DIFFERENT TYPES OF VEGAN DIETS

There are different varieties of vegan diets. The most common include:

Whole-food vegan diet: A diet based on a wide variety of whole plant foods such as fruits, vegetables, whole grains, legumes, nuts and seeds.

Raw-food vegan diet: A vegan diet based on raw fruits, vegetables, nuts, seeds or plant foods cooked at temperatures below 118°F (48°C)

80/10/10: The 80/10/10 diet is a raw-food vegan diet that limits fat-rich plants such as nuts and avocados and relies mainly on raw fruits and soft greens instead. Also referred to as the low-fat, raw-food vegan diet or fruitarian diet.

The starch solution: A low-fat, high-carb vegan diet similar to the 80/10/10 but that focuses on cooked starches like potatoes, rice and corn instead of fruit.

Raw till 4: A low-fat vegan diet inspired by the 80/10/10 and starch solution. Raw foods are consumed until 4 p.m., with the option of a cooked plant-based meal for dinner.

The thrive diet: The thrive diet is a raw-food vegan diet. Followers eat plant-based, whole foods that are raw or minimally cooked at low temperatures.

Junk-food vegan diet: A vegan diet lacking in whole plant foods that relies heavily on mock meats and cheeses, fries, vegan desserts and other heavily processed vegan foods.

Although several variations of the vegan diet exist, most scientific research rarely differentiates between different types of vegan diets

Vegan Diets Can Help You Lose Weight

Vegans tend to be thinner and have a lower body mass index (BMI) than non-vegans This might explain why an increasing number of people turn to vegan diets as a way to lose excess weight.

Part of the weight-related benefits vegans experience may be explained by factors other than diet. These may include healthier lifestyle choices, such as physical activity, and other health-related behaviors.

However, several randomized controlled studies, which control for these external factors, report that vegan diets are more effective for weight loss than the diets they are compared to

Interestingly, the weight loss advantage persists even when whole-food-based diets are used as control diets.

These include diets recommended by the American Dietetics Association (ADA), the American Heart Association (AHA) and the National Cholesterol Education Program (NCEP)

What's more, researchers generally report that participants on vegan diets lose more weight than those following calorie-restricted diets, even when they're allowed to eat until they feel full

The natural tendency to eat fewer calories on a vegan diet may be caused by a higher dietary fiber intake, which can make you feel fuller.

Vegan Diets, Blood Sugar and Type 2 Diabetes

Adopting a vegan diet may help keep your blood sugar in check and type 2 diabetes at bay.

Several studies show that vegans benefit from lower blood sugar levels, higher insulin sensitivity and up to a 78% lower risk of developing type 2 diabetes than non-vegans

In addition, vegan diets reportedly lower blood sugar levels in diabetics up to 2.4 times more than diets recommended by the ADA, AHA and NCEP Part of the advantage could be explained by the higher fiber intake, which may blunt the blood sugar response. A vegan diet's weight loss effects may further contribute to its ability to lower blood sugar levels

# VEGAN DIETS AND HEART HEALTH

A vegan diet may help keep your heart healthy.

Observational studies report vegans may have up to a 75% lower risk of developing high blood pressure and 42% lower risk of dying from heart disease

Randomized controlled studies — the gold standard in research — add to the evidence.

Several report that vegan diets are much more effective at reducing blood sugar, LDL and total cholesterol than diets they are compared to

These effects could be especially beneficial since reducing blood pressure, cholesterol and blood sugar may reduce heart disease risk by up to 46%

Other Health Benefits of Vegan Diets

Vegan diets are linked to an array of other health benefits, including benefits for:

Cancer risk: Vegans may benefit from a 15% lower risk of developing or dying from cancer (20Trusted Source).

Arthritis: Vegan diets seem particularly effective at reducing symptoms of arthritis such as pain, joint swelling and morning stiffness

Kidney function: Diabetics who substitute meat for plant protein may reduce their risk of poor kidney function Alzheimer's disease: Observational studies show that aspects of the vegan diet may help reduce the risk of developing Alzheimer's disease

That said, keep in mind that most of the studies supporting these benefits are observational. This makes it difficult to determine whether the vegan diet directly caused the benefits.

Randomized controlled studies are needed before strong conclusions can be made.

# FOODS TO AVOID

Vegans avoid eating any animal foods, as well as any foods containing ingredients derived from animals. These include:

Meat and poultry: Beef, lamb, pork, veal, horse, organ meat, wild meat, chicken, turkey, goose, duck, quail, etc.

Fish and seafood: All types of fish, anchovies, shrimp, squid, scallops, calamari, mussels, crab, lobster, etc.

Dairy: Milk, yogurt, cheese, butter, cream, ice cream, etc.

Eggs: From chickens, quails, ostriches, fish, etc.

Bee products: Honey, bee pollen, royal jelly, etc.

Animal-based ingredients: Whey, casein, lactose, egg white albumen, gelatin, cochineal or carmine, isinglass, shellac, L-cysteine, animal-derived vitamin D3 and fish-derived omega-3 fatty acids.

Foods to Eat

Health-conscious vegans substitute animal products with plant-based replacements, such as:

Tofu, tempeh and seitan: These provide a versatile protein-rich alternative to meat, fish, poultry and eggs in many recipes.

Legumes: Foods such as beans, lentils and peas are excellent sources of many nutrients and beneficial plant compounds. Sprouting, fermenting and proper cooking can increase nutrient absorption (34Trusted Source).

Nuts and nut butters: Especially unblanched and unroasted varieties, which are good sources of iron, fiber, magnesium, zinc, selenium and vitamin E

Seeds: Especially hemp, chia and flaxseeds, which contain a good amount of protein and beneficial omega-3 fatty acids

Calcium-fortified plant milks and yogurts: These help vegans achieve their recommended dietary calcium intakes. Opt for varieties also fortified with vitamins B12 and D whenever possible.

Algae: Spirulina and chlorella are good sources of complete protein. Other varieties are great sources of iodine.

Nutritional yeast: This is an easy way to increase the protein content of vegan dishes and add an interesting cheesy flavor. Pick vitamin B12-fortified varieties whenever possible.

Whole grains, cereals and pseudocereals: These are a great source of complex carbs, fiber, iron, B-vitamins and several minerals. Spelt, teff, amaranth and quinoa are especially high-protein options Sprouted and fermented plant foods: Ezekiel bread, tempeh, miso, natto, sauerkraut, pickles, kimchi and kombucha often contain probiotics and vitamin K2. Sprouting and fermenting can also help improve mineral absorption

Fruits and vegetables: Both are great foods to increase your nutrient intake. Leafy greens such as bok choy, spinach, kale, watercress and mustard greens are particularly high in iron and calcium.

Risks and How to Minimize Them

Favoring a well-planned diet that limits processed foods and replaces them with nutrient-rich ones instead is important for everyone, not only vegans.

That said, those following poorly planned vegan diets are particularly at risk of certain nutrient deficiencies.

In fact, studies show that vegans are at a higher risk of having inadequate blood levels of vitamin B12, vitamin D, long-chain omega-3s, iodine, iron, calcium and zinc Not getting enough of these nutrients is worrisome for everyone, but it may pose a particular risk to those with increased requirements, such as children or women who are pregnant or breastfeeding.

Your genetic makeup and the composition of your gut bacteria may also influence your ability to derive the nutrients you need from a vegan diet.

One way to minimize the likelihood of deficiency is to limit the amount of processed vegan foods you consume and opt for nutrient-rich plant foods instead.

Fortified foods, especially those enriched with calcium, vitamin D and vitamin B12, should also make a daily appearance on your plate.

Furthermore, vegans wanting to enhance their absorption of iron and zinc should try fermenting, sprouting and cooking foods

Also, the use of iron cast pots and pans for cooking, avoiding tea or coffee with meals and combining iron-rich foods with a source of vitamin C can further boost iron absorption

Moreover, the addition of seaweed or iodized salt to the diet can help vegans reach their recommended daily intake of iodine

Lastly, omega-3 containing foods, especially those high in alpha-linolenic acid (ALA), can help the body produce longer-chain omega-3s such as eicosapentaenoic acid (EPA) and docosahexaenoic acid (DHA).

Foods high in ALA include chia, hemp, flaxseeds, walnuts and soybeans. However, there's debate regarding whether this conversion is efficient enough to meet daily needs

Therefore, a daily intake of 200–300 mg of EPA and DHA from an algae oil supplement may be a safer way to prevent low levels

# SUPPLEMENTS TO CONSIDER

Some vegans may find it difficult to eat enough of the nutrient-rich or fortified foods above to meet their daily requirements.

In this case, the following supplements can be particularly beneficial:

Vitamin B12: Vitamin B12 in cyanocobalamin form is the most studied and seems to work well for most people (62Trusted Source).

Vitamin D: Opt for D2 or vegan D3 forms such as those manufactured by Nordic Naturals or Viridian.

EPA and DHA: Sourced from algae oil.

Iron: Should only be supplemented in the case of a documented deficiency. Ingesting too much iron from supplements can cause health complications and prevent the absorption of other nutrients (63Trusted Source).

Iodine: Take a supplement or add 1/2 teaspoon of iodized salt to your diet daily.

Calcium: Calcium is best absorbed when taken in doses of 500 mg or less at a time. Taking calcium at the same time as iron or zinc supplements may reduce their absorption

Zinc: Taken in zinc gluconate or zinc citrate forms. Not to be taken at the same time as calcium supplements (64).

Zinc: Taken in zinc gluconate or zinc citrate forms. Not to be taken at the same time as calcium supplements (64).

# A VEGAN SAMPLE MENU FOR ONE WEEK

To help get you started, here's a simple plan covering a week's worth of vegan meals:

Monday

Breakfast: Vegan breakfast sandwich with tofu, lettuce, tomato, turmeric and a plant-milk chai latte.

Lunch: Spiralized zucchini and quinoa salad with peanut dressing.

Dinner: Red lentil and spinach dal over wild rice.

Tuesday

Breakfast: Overnight oats made with fruit, fortified plant milk, chia seeds and nuts.

Lunch: Seitan sauerkraut sandwich.

Dinner: Pasta with a lentil bolognese sauce and a side salad.

Wednesday

Breakfast: Mango and spinach smoothie made with

fortified plant milk and a banana-flaxseed-walnut muffin.

Lunch: Baked tofu sandwich with a side of tomato salad.

Dinner: Vegan chili on a bed of amaranth.

Thursday

Breakfast: Whole-grain toast with hazelnut butter, banana and a fortified plant yogurt.

Lunch: Tofu noodle soup with vegetables.

Dinner: Jacket sweet potatoes with lettuce, corn, beans, cashews and guacamole.

Friday

Breakfast: Vegan chickpea and onion omelet and a cappuccino made with fortified plant milk.

Lunch: Vegan tacos with mango-pineapple salsa.

Dinner: Tempeh stir-fry with bok choy and broccoli.

Saturday

Breakfast: Spinach and scrambled tofu wrap and a glass of fortified plant milk.

Lunch: Spiced red lentil, tomato and kale soup with whole-grain toast and hummus.

Dinner: Veggie sushi rolls, miso soup, edamame and wakame salad.

Sunday

Breakfast: Chickpea pancakes, guacamole and salsa and a glass of fortified orange juice.

Lunch: Tofu vegan quiche with a side of sautéed mustard greens.

Dinner: Vegan spring rolls.

Remember to vary your sources of protein and vegetables throughout the day, as each provides different vitamins and minerals that are important for your health.

# HOW TO EAT VEGAN AT RESTAURANTS

When dining in a non-vegan establishment, try scanning the menu online beforehand to see what vegan options they may have for you.

Sometimes, calling ahead of time allows the chef to arrange something especially for you. This permits you to arrive at the restaurant confident that you'll have something hopefully more interesting than a side salad to order.

When picking a restaurant on the fly, make sure to ask about their vegan options as soon as you step in, ideally before being seated.

When in doubt, opt for ethnic restaurants. They tend to have dishes that are naturally vegan-friendly or can be easily modified to become so. Mexican, Thai, Middle-Eastern, Ethiopian and Indian restaurants tend to be great options.

Once in the restaurant, try identifying the vegetarian options on the menu and asking whether the dairy or eggs can be removed to make the dish vegan-friendly.

Healthy Vegan Snacks

Snacks are a great way to stay energized and keep hunger at bay between meals.

Some interesting, portable vegan options include:

Fresh fruit with a dollop of nut butter

Hummus and vegetables

Nutritional yeast sprinkled on popcorn

Roasted chickpeas

Nut and fruit bars

Trail mix

Chia pudding

Homemade muffins

Whole-wheat pita with salsa and guacamole

Cereal with plant milk

Edamame

Whole-grain crackers and cashew nut spread

A plant-milk latte or cappuccino

Dried seaweed snacks

Whenever planning a vegan snack, try to opt for fiber- and protein-rich options, which can help keep hunger away.

Frequently Asked Questions

Here are some frequently asked questions about veganism.

1. Can I only eat raw food as a vegan?

Absolutely not. Although some vegans choose to do so, raw veganism isn't for everyone. Many vegans eat cooked food, and there is no scientific basis for you to eat only raw foods.

2. Will switching to a vegan diet help me lose weight?

A vegan diet that emphasizes nutritious, whole plant foods and limits processed ones may help you lose weight.

As mentioned in the weight loss section above, vegan diets tend to help people eat fewer calories without having to consciously restrict their food intake.

That said, when matched for calories, vegan diets are no more effective than other diets for weight loss

3. What is the best milk substitute?

There are many plant-based milk alternatives to cow's milk. Soy and hemp varieties contain more protein, making them more beneficial to those trying to keep their protein intake high.

Whichever plant milk you choose, ensure it's enriched with calcium, vitamin D and, if possible, vitamin B12.

4. Vegans tend to eat a lot of soy. Is this bad for you?

Soybeans are great sources of plant-based protein. They

contain an array of vitamins, minerals, antioxidants and beneficial plant compounds that are linked to various health benefits

However, soy may suppress thyroid function in predisposed individuals and cause gas and diarrhea in others

It's best to opt for minimally processed soy food products such as tofu and edamame and limit the use of soy-based mock meats.

Fermented soy products such as tempeh and natto are especially beneficial, as fermentation helps improve the absorption of nutrients

5. How can I replace eggs in recipes?

Chia and flax seeds are a great way to replace eggs in baking. To replace one egg, simply mix one tablespoon of chia or ground flaxseeds with three tablespoons of hot water and allow it to rest until it gels.

Mashed bananas can also be a great alternative to eggs in some cases.

Scrambled tofu is a good vegan alternative to scrambled eggs. Tofu can also be used in a variety of egg-based recipes ranging from omelets to frittatas and quiches.

6. How can I make sure I get enough protein?

Vegans can ensure they meet their daily protein requirements by including protein-rich plant foods in their daily meals.

7. How can I make sure I get enough calcium?

Calcium-rich foods include bok choy, kale, mustard

greens, turnip greens, watercress, broccoli, chickpeas and calcium-set tofu.

Fortified plant milks and juices are also a great way for vegans to increase their calcium intake.

The RDA for calcium is 1,000 mg per day for most adults and increases to 1,200 mg per day for adults over 50 years old

Some argue that vegans may have slightly lower daily requirements because of the lack of meat in their diets. Not much scientific evidence can be found to support or negate this claim.

However, current studies show that vegans consuming less than 525 mg of calcium each day have an increased risk of bone fractures

8. Should I take a vitamin B12 supplement?

Vitamin B12 is generally found in animal foods. Some plant foods may contain a form of this vitamin, but there's still debate about whether this form is active in humans

Despite circulating rumors, there's no scientific evidence to support unwashed produce as a reliable source of vitamin B12.

The daily recommended intake is 2.4 mcg per day for adults, 2.6 mcg per day during pregnancy and 2.8 mcg per day while breastfeeding

Vitamin B12-fortified products and supplements are the only two reliable forms of vitamin B12 for vegans.

Unfortunately, many vegans seem to fail to consume

sufficient vitamin B12 to meet their daily requirements

If you're unable to meet your daily requirements through the use of vitamin B12-fortified products, you should definitely consider taking a vitamin B12 supplement.

# SUPPLEMENTS YOU NEED ON A VEGAN DIET

. Vitamin B12

Foods often touted to be rich in vitamin B12 include un-washed organic produce, mushrooms grown in B12-rich soils, nori, spirulina, chlorella, and nutritional yeast.

Some believe vegans who eat enough of the right plant foods don't need to worry about vitamin B12 deficiency.

However, there is no scientific basis for this belief.

Several studies show that while anyone can have low vitamin B12 levels, vegetarians and vegans have a higher risk of deficiency. This seems especially true for vegans who are not taking any supplements

Vitamin B12 is important for many bodily processes, including protein metabolism and the formation of oxygen-transporting red blood cells. It also plays a crucial role in the health of your nervous system

Too little vitamin B12 can lead to anemia and nervous system damage, as well as infertility and bone and heart disease

The daily recommended intake is 2.4 mcg per day for adults, 2.6 mcg per day during pregnancy, and 2.8 mcg per day while breastfeeding.

The only scientifically proven way for vegans to reach these levels is by consuming B12-fortified foods or taking a vitamin B12 supplement. B12-fortified foods commonly include plant milks, soy products, breakfast cereals, and nutritional yeast.

Some plant foods seem to contain a form of vitamin B12 naturally, but there's still debate on whether this form is active in humans

What's more, no scientific evidence supports depending on unwashed organic produce as a reliable source of vitamin B12.

Nutritional yeast only contains vitamin B12 when fortified. However, vitamin B12 is light-sensitive and may degrade if bought from or stored in clear plastic bags

It's important to keep in mind that vitamin B12 is best absorbed in small doses. Thus, the less frequently you ingest vitamin B12, the more you need to take.

This is why vegans who are unable to reach the recommended daily intake using fortified foods should opt for a daily supplement providing 25–100 mcg of cyanocobalamin or a weekly dosage of 2,000 mcg.

Those wary of taking supplements may find it reassuring to get their blood levels of vitamin B12 checked before taking any.

Finally, your ability to absorb vitamin B12 decreases with

age. Therefore, the Institute of Medicine recommends that everyone over the age of 51 — vegan or not — consider fortified foods or a vitamin B12 supplement

2. Vitamin D

Vitamin D is a fat-soluble vitamin that helps enhance the absorption of calcium and phosphorus from your gut

This vitamin also influences many other bodily processes, including immune function, mood, memory, and muscle recovery

The recommended daily allowance (RDA) for vitamin D for children and adults is 600 IU (15 mcg) per day. The elderly, as well as pregnant or lactating women, should aim for 800 IU (20 mcg) per day (22).

That said, some evidence suggests that your daily requirements are far greater than the current RDA

Unfortunately, very few foods naturally contain vitamin D, and foods fortified with vitamin D are often considered insufficient to satisfy the daily requirements.

This could partly explain the worldwide reports of vitamin D deficiency among vegans and omnivores alike

Aside from the small amount you get from your diet, vitamin D can be made from sun exposure. Most people likely make enough vitamin D by spending 15 minutes in the midday sun when the sun is strong — as long as they don't use any sunscreen and expose most of their skin.

However, the elderly, people with darker skin, those who live in northern latitudes or colder climates, and those who spend little time outdoors may be unable to produce enough

Furthermore, because of the known negative effects of excess UV radiation, many dermatologists warn against using sun exposure to boost vitamin D levels

The best way vegans can ensure they're getting enough vitamin D is to have their blood levels tested. Those unable to get enough from fortified foods and sunshine should consider taking a daily vitamin D2 or vegan vitamin D3 supplement.

Although vitamin D2 is probably adequate for most people, some studies suggest that vitamin D3 is more effective at raising blood levels of vitamin D

3. Long-chain omega-3s

Omega-3 fatty acids can be split into two categories:

Essential omega-3 fatty acids: Alpha-linolenic acid (ALA) is the only essential omega-3 fatty acid, meaning you can only get it from your diet.

Long-chain omega-3 fatty acids: This category includes eicosapentaenoic acid (EPA) and docosahexaenoic acid (DHA). They are not considered essential because your body can make them from ALA.

Long-chain omega-3 fatty acids play a structural role in your brain and eyes. Adequate dietary levels also seem important for brain development and reducing the risk of inflammation, depression, breast cancer, and attention deficit hyperactivity disorder (ADHD)

Plants with a high ALA content include flax seeds, chia seeds, walnuts, hemp seeds, and soybeans. EPA and DHA are mostly found in animal products like fatty fish and fish oil.

Getting enough ALA should theoretically maintain adequate EPA and DHA levels. However, studies estimate that the conversion of ALA to EPA may be as low as 5–10%, while its conversion to DHA may be near 2–5% (37Trusted Source, 38Trusted Source).

Additionally, research consistently shows that vegetarians and vegans have up to 50% lower blood and tissue concentrations of EPA and DHA than omnivores

Most health professionals agree that 200–300 mg per day should be sufficient

Vegans can reach this recommended intake by supplementing with algae oil.

What's more, minimizing your intake of omega-6 fatty acids from oils, including corn, safflower, sunflower, and sesame oils, as well as making sure to eat enough ALA-rich foods, may further help maximize EPA and DHA levels

4. Iodine

Getting enough iodine is crucial for healthy thyroid function, which controls your metabolism.

An iodine deficiency during pregnancy and early infancy can result in irreversible intellectual disability

In adults, insufficient iodine intake can lead to hypothyroidism.

This can cause various symptoms, such as low energy levels, dry skin, tingling in your hands and feet, forgetfulness, depression, and weight gain

Vegans are considered at risk of iodine deficiency, and studies report that vegans have up to 50% lower blood iodine levels than vegetarians

The RDA for adults is 150 mcg of iodine per day. Pregnant women should aim for 220 mcg per day, while those who are breastfeeding are recommended to further increase their daily intake to 290 mcg per day

Iodine levels in plant foods depend on the iodine content of the soil in which they were grown. For instance, food grown close to the ocean tends to be higher in iodine.

The only foods considered to have consistently high iodine levels are iodized salt, seafood, seaweed, and dairy products, which pick up iodine from solutions used to clean cows and farm equipment.

Half a teaspoon (2.5 ml) of iodized salt is sufficient to meet your daily needs.

Vegans who do not want to consume iodized salt or eat seaweed several times per week should consider taking an iodine supplement.

5. Iron

Iron is a nutrient used to make new DNA and red blood cells, as well as carry oxygen in the blood. It's also needed for energy metabolism

Too little iron can lead to anemia and symptoms like fatigue nd decreased immune function.

The RDA is 8 mg for adult men and post-menopausal

women. It increases to 18 mg per day for adult women, and pregnant women should aim for 27 mg per day

Iron can be found in two forms: heme and non-heme. Heme iron is only available from animal products, whereas non-heme iron is found in plants

Because heme iron is more easily absorbed from your diet than non-heme iron, vegans are often recommended to aim for 1.8 times the normal RDA. That said, more studies are needed to establish whether such high intakes are needed

Vegans with a low iron intake should aim to eat more iron-rich foods, such as cruciferous vegetables, beans, peas, dried fruit, nuts, and seeds. Iron-fortified foods, such as cereals, enriched breads, and some plant milks, can further help

Also, using cast-iron pots and pans to cook, avoiding tea or coffee with meals, and combining iron-rich foods with a source of vitamin C can help boost iron absorption.

The best way to determine whether supplements are necessary is to get your hemoglobin and ferritin levels checked by your health practitioner.

Unnecessary intake of supplements like iron can do more harm than good by damaging cells or blocking the absorption of other minerals

Extremely high levels can even cause convulsions, lead to organ failure or coma, and be fatal in some cases. Thus, it's best not to supplement unless it's truly necessary

6. Calcium

Calcium is a mineral that's necessary for good bone and teeth health. It also plays a role in muscle function, nerve signaling, and heart health.

The RDA for calcium is set at 1,000 mg per day for most adults and increases to 1,200 mg per day for adults over the age of 50

Plant sources of calcium include bok choy, kale, mustard greens, turnip greens, watercress, broccoli, chickpeas, calcium-set tofu, and fortified plant milks or juices.

However, studies tend to agree that most vegans don't get enough calcium An often-heard remark among the vegan community is that vegans have lower calcium needs than omnivores because they do not use this mineral to neutralize the acidity produced by a meat-rich diet.

More research is needed to evaluate how meatless diets affect daily calcium requirements. However, evidence suggests that vegans consuming less than 525 mg of calcium tend to have an increased risk of bone fractures

For this reason, all vegans are encouraged to aim for the RDA, making sure they consume at least 525 mg of calcium per day. Supplements should be used if this can't be achieved through diet or fortified foods alone.

7. Zinc

Zinc is a mineral that's crucial for metabolism, immune function, and the repair of body cells.

An insufficient intake of zinc can lead to developmental problems, hair loss, diarrhea, and delayed wound healing.

The RDA for zinc is currently set at 8–11 mg per day for

adults. It increases to 11–12 mg for pregnant women and 12–13 mg for lactating women

Few plant foods contain high amounts of zinc. Moreover, zinc absorption from some plant foods is limited due to their phytate content. Thus, vegetarians are encouraged to aim for 1.5 times the RDA

While not all vegans have low blood levels of zinc, a recent review of 26 studies showed that vegetarians — and especially vegans — have lower zinc intakes and slightly lower blood levels of zinc than omnivores

To maximize your intake, eat a variety of zinc-rich foods throughout the day. These include whole grains, wheat germ, tofu, sprouted breads, legumes, nuts, and seeds.

Soaking nuts, seeds, and legumes overnight, eating enough protein, and consuming fermented foods, such as tempeh and miso, also seems to boost absorption

Vegans concerned about their zinc intake or those with symptoms of a deficiency may consider taking a daily zinc gluconate or zinc citrate supplement that provides 50–100% of the RDA.

# THUG KICTHEN VEGAN DIET RECIPES

Lentil and Potato Stew

Ingredients

2 teaspoons olive oil

1 small onion, chopped

500 grams / 2 cups potatoes, cut into 2cm pieces

250 grams / 1 1/2 cups carrots, cut into 1 cm slices

4 cloves garlic, minced

1 tablespoon rosemary leaves, finely chopped*

1 teaspoon sea salt, to taste

1 teaspoon pepper

1/2 teaspoon paprika

1/4 teaspoon cayenne pepper

1 tablespoon apple cider vinegar

750 ml / 3 cups vegetable stock

150 grams / 1 cup brown lentils, soaked if possible**

1 teaspoon coconut sugar or honey***

1/2 teaspoon dijon mustard

3 tablespoons thyme, finely chopped

70 grams / 3 cups rucola (arugula) or other greens****

Instructions

In a large pot, heat the oil over medium. Add the onion and sauté for a couple of minutes or until softened and fragrant. Stir in the potatoes and carrots and cook for another five minutes, stirring occasionally, to brown slightly.

Add the garlic and rosemary, cook for an additional minute, then add the spices and stir for about 30 seconds. Pour the apple cider vinegar into the pot and stir, then the stock.

Increase the heat to high and bring the stew to a rolling boil. Add the lentils and reduce the heat to medium-low, then simmer for 25-30 minutes, or until the carrots and potatoes are tender.

Take the pot off the heat and stir in the coconut sugar, mustard, thyme, and greens. Serve hot and keep leftovers in the fridge for up to 3 days. The stew will thicken slightly as it sits.

# BBQ CHICKPEA COLLARD WRAPS

INGREDIENTS:

TANGY CABBAGE SLAW

4 cups shredded cabbage (about 1 small head)

2 cups shredded carrots (about 6 large carrots)

2 small green apples, cored and sliced into matchsticks (optional)

2 tablespoons apple cider vinegar

2 tablespoons lime juice (about 1 small lime)

salt to taste

BBQ CHICKPEA WRAPS

8 collard green leaves

1 (15-ounce) can chickpeas, drained

1 cup cooked quinoa (optional)*

1/2 cup homemade vegan BBQ sauce (or your favorite store-bought sauce)

hemp ranch dressing for serving

## DIRECTIONS:

In a large bowl, combine the ingredients for the cabbage slaw. Stir together until evenly coated then set aside.

Thoroughly rinse and dry the collard leaves, slice off the bottom stem, then set face down. Using a sharp knife, carefully shave off the thick part of stem on the inside of the wrap. It works best if you slice from the top of the leaf working toward the bottom. This step will make it easier to fold into a wrap.

In a small saucepan over medium-low heat (I used the same one that I cooked the quinoa in), combine the chickpeas and the cooked quinoa. Add the barbecue sauce to the saucepan then stir together until evenly coated. Cook for 5 minutes, until heated through.

Scoop 1/8th of the chickpea mixture into the center of each collard leaf along with the cabbage slaw.  Fold in the top and bottom sides then gently roll like you would a burrito. Serve with hemp ranch dressing and enjoy!

*I like to add quinoa for extra protein but you can skip it if you're short on time. However, please note that it will decrease the serving size to 6 wraps. To make 1 cup cooked quinoa, combine 1/2 cup dry quinoa with 1 cup water and a dash of salt. Bring to a boil over medium-high heat then decrease the heat to a gentle simmer. Cook until the quinoa has absorbed all of the water, about 10 minutes. Remove the pot from heat, cover, and let the quinoa steam for 5 minutes.

If not using the quinoa you can also roast the chickpeas on a lined baking sheet in the oven for 10 minutes at 400°F then transfer them to a bowl with 1/4 cup barbecue sauce instead of 1/2 cup.

# ROASTED CAULIFLOWER & BRUSSELS SPROUTS

Ingredients

1 small head cauliflower, cut into florets (I used purple cauliflower found at Whole Foods)

1 pound brussels sprouts, larger pieces sliced in half

6 garlic cloves, peeled and crushed

6 sprigs thyme

salt and pepper

2-3 tablespoons melted coconut oil or avocado oil

1-2 tablespoons balsamic vinegar

Instructions

Preheat oven to 400F. Place cauliflower, brussels sprouts, and garlic onto a large baking sheet. Remove thyme leaves from their stems and sprinkle over the vegetables. Drizzle with oil and toss mixture together to evenly coat and sprinkle with plenty of salt and pepper.

Place pan into the preheated oven and bake for 25-35 minutes. Remove pan after about 15-20 minutes and toss vegetables with balsamic vinegar. Return to the oven to finish baking.

May need more or less time, depending on the size of your vegetables. Keep a close eye after 20-25 minutes minutes to prevent burning.

## FAT-BUSTING VEGETARIAN COLLARD GREENS SOUP

Ingredients

1 Tbs olive oil

2 tsp smoked paprika

1 tsp chili powder

1 tsp cumin

pinch red pepper flakes

1 onion, chopped

3 large carrots, sliced

3 stalks celery, chopped

10 cups water

15 oz. can no-salt-added diced tomatoes

6 oz. can no-salt-added tomato paste

2 Tbs lower sodium tamari or soy sauce

2 Tbs lemon juice

1 Tbs salt-free herb seasoning (I like Mrs. Dash)

1 Tbs sugar/sweetener, your choice (see recipe notes)

1 tsp roasted garlic granules or garlic powder

1/2 tsp salt

fresh black pepper to taste

1 cup dried lentils

6 cups packed collard greens, stems removed

1/4 cup uncooked quinoa

Instructions

Prep the veggies and greens.

Add the oil to a large, lidded cooking pot.

Add the paprika, chili powder, cumin and red pepper flakes.

Raise the heat to medium.

Add the onion, carrots and celery. Saute about 10 minutes.

Add the water, tomatoes, paste, tamari or soy sauce, lemon juice, herb seasoning, sweetener, garlic granules, salt, pepper and lentils. Stir to combine.

Stir in the collard greens.

Raise the heat to medium high. Bring to a boil.

Cover and turn the heat down to a simmer.

Simmer for 30 minutes, stirring occasionally.

Stir in the quinoa.

Simmer another 15-20 minutes.

# SLOW COOKER MASHED POTATOES & CRANBERRY MUSHROOM SAUCE

Vegan, Vegetarian, Gluten-Free

Ingredients

2 large potatoes2 large potatoes

1 1/2 cups unsweetened plain almond milk1 1/2 cups unsweetened plain almond milk

1 tsp crushed garlic1 tsp crushed garlic

salt/peppersalt/pepper

1 tsp coconut oil1 tsp coconut oil

2 cups mushrooms2 cups mushrooms

1 1/2 cups spinach1 1/2 cups spinach

1/4 cup organic cranberry sauce1/4 cup organic cranberry sauce

Instructions

Peel and cut the potatoes into small slices.

Place the potatoes in the slow cooker. Add 3/4 cups of almond milk, garlic, and salt/pepper.

Cook on high for about 2 hours, stirring every 30 minutes to keep them from sticking to the sides.

When the potatoes have about 30 minutes left, heat the coconut oil in a pan over medium heat. Add in the mushrooms and sauté for about 5-7 minutes. Add in the spinach and lightly sauté. Remove from pan and set aside.

Heat up the cranberry sauce in the same pan. Set aside.

Using a potato masher or a stand mixer, mash the potatoes. Add in the remaining almond milk and continue to mash to desired texture.

Serve mashed potatoes in two bowls, topping with the sautéed mushrooms, spinach, and cranberry sauce. Enjoy!

# ROASTED BROCCOLINI WITH MUSHROOMS IN BALSAMIC SAUCE

Ingredients:

1 lb broccolini (2 bunches) - ends trimmed

Olive oil

1 shallot - finely sliced

1/2 lb your choice of mushrooms - thinly sliced (I used baby portobello mushrooms)

A dab of unsalted butter

2 tbsp balsamic vinegar

3 tbsp vegetable or chicken broth

A swirl of dry white wine or marsala wine (optional)

Sea salt ( try our Ginger-Lime Sea Salt)

Season with Spice's Aleppo Chili Flakes

Method:

1. Preheat oven to 400°F.

2. Place the broccolini on a baking sheet. Drizzle on some olive oil, sprinkle lightly with sea salt (our Ginger-Lime Sea Salt works really well here), and toss to coat evenly. Then spread the broccolini in a single layer.

3. Roast the broccolini for about 12 - 15 minutes, or until tender-crisp (turning over once). Transfer the broccolini to a platter.

4. While the broccolini is roasting, heat about 2 tbsp of olive oil in a large skillet or frying pan over medium heat. Add in the sliced shallot and saute until they begin to soften.

5. Turn heat to medium-high, add in the mushrooms and a pinch of sea salt. Saute the mushrooms for about 8 to 10 minutes. The mushrooms will start to release some moisture and once it begins to evaporate, add in a dab of butter. Stir, then add in the balsamic vinegar and broth. Continue to cook for a minute. Swirl in dry white wine or marsala wine (if using), and saute for another 2-3 minutes - until the liquid cooks down. Sprinkle in a bit more sea salt.

6. Serve the mushrooms over the roasted broccolini, then sprinkle the Aleppo Chili Flakes on top. Serve warm.


Vegan Vegetable Barley Soup

Ingredients

1 cup uncooked pearl barley1 cup uncooked pearl barley

3-4 tbsp vegetable broth to saute (or water)3-4 tbsp vegetable broth to saute (or water)

1 large yellow onion diced1 large yellow onion diced

4 medium garlic cloves minced4 medium garlic cloves minced

2 large celery stalks sliced2 large celery stalks sliced

1 ½ tbsp Italian seasonings1 ½ tbsp Italian seasonings

1 tsp paprika1 tsp paprika

1 tsp dried parsley peeled and diced1 tsp dried parsley peeled and diced

½ tsp chili pepper flakes peeled and sliced½ tsp chili pepper flakes peeled and sliced

1 medium bay leaf1 medium bay leaf

¾ tsp salt¾ tsp salt

½ tsp black pepper½ tsp black pepper

3 cups russet potatoes peeled and diced3 cups russet potatoes peeled and diced

4 cups frozen mixed vegetables (I used a mix of corn, peas, carrots, and green beans)4 cups frozen mixed vegetables (I used a mix of corn, peas, carrots, and green beans)

14 oz can diced tomatoes with the juice14 oz can diced tomatoes with the juice

4 cups vegetable broth4 cups vegetable broth

1 cup water1 cup water

8 oz frozen spinach8 oz frozen spinach

2 tbsp lemon juice2 tbsp lemon juice

Instructions

Cook the barley according to the package instructions, drain any excess water, and then set it aside for later.

In a large dutch oven, saute the diced onion and sliced celery in vegetable broth over medium heat until soft. Add the minced garlic, 1 ½ tbsp Italian seasonings, 1 tsp paprika, 1 tsp dried parsley, ½ tsp chili pepper flakes, bay leaf, ¾ tsp salt, and ½ tsp black pepper to the pot. Stir to combine and let it cook for 2 minutes to toast the spices.

Add the potatoes, frozen mixed vegetables, diced tomatoes with juice, 4 cups vegetable broth, and 1 cup water to the pot. Increase the heat and bring it to a simmer and then reduce the heat to medium. Cover it and let it cook for 30 minutes or until the potatoes are tender.

Stir in the frozen spinach and lemon juice. Let it cook for about 5 minutes or until the spinach is fully defrosted and warmed through. Taste and add more salt and pepper if necessary. Remove and discard the bay leaf.

Add a scoop of the cooked barley to a bowl and then ladle the hot soup over the top and stir to incorporate the barley. Garnish with dried parsley before serving.

Notes

I recommend cooking the barley separately so it doesn't absorb all of the broth. If you'd rather cook it in the soup, make sure you add an additional 3 cups of water or broth for it to absorb while it cooks.

Wait to add the frozen spinach until the last few minutes of cooking. You don't need to "cook" the spinach, we're just trying to defrost and warm it. I like to add it at the end of cooking so it keeps its bright green color.

Store leftovers in an airtight container in the fridge for 4-5 days or you can freeze it for a future meal.

# VEGAN WINTER SALAD

INGREDIENTS

SALAD

¼ cauliflower

2 celery sticks

a wedge of red cabbage

a small turnip

2 carrots

1 green apple

25 g / 1 oz baby spinach

25 g / 1 oz rocket

fresh parsley, finely chopped

¼ cup almonds

¼ cup pomegranate seeds OR dried cranberries

DRESSING

2 tbsp extra virgin olive oil

2 tbsp pomegranate molasses

1 small garlic clove, grated finely

salt and pepper, to taste

METHOD

Chop almonds diagonally. Put a small frying pan on a medium heat and dry roast almonds until lightly browned and fragrant. Make sure you move them around the pan frequently as they burn easily.

Whisk all the dressing ingredients together in a small bowl. Season with salt and pepper to taste.

Wash your apple, celery sticks, cauliflower, spinach and rocket well and pat them dry. Peel the carrots and the turnip. Using a mandolin slicer shred the cabbage on the thinnest setting, slice carrots and turnip on the same setting too. Cut apples, celery sticks and raw cauliflower into slightly thicker slices with a sharp knife.

Mix all the vegetables together with dry rocket, baby spinach and chopped parsley in a mixing bowl. Dress and season well.

Transfer to a serving bowl. Sprinkle the salad with toasted almonds and pomegranate seeds (or cranberries).

Spaghetti Squash Burrito Bowls

INGREDIENTS

Roasted spaghetti squash

2 medium spaghetti squash (about 2 pounds each), halved and seeds removed

2 tablespoons olive oil

Salt and freshly ground black pepper

Cabbage and black bean slaw

2 cups purple cabbage, thinly sliced and roughly chopped into 2-inch long pieces

1 can (15 ounces) black beans, rinsed and drained

1 red bell pepper, chopped

1/3 cup chopped green onions, both green and white parts

1/3 cup chopped fresh cilantro

2 to 3 tablespoons fresh lime juice, to taste

1 teaspoon olive oil

1/4 teaspoon salt

Avocado salsa verde

3/4 cup mild salsa verde, either homemade or store-bought

1 ripe avocado, diced

1/3 cup fresh cilantro (a few stems are ok)

1 tablespoon fresh lime juice

1 medium garlic clove, roughly chopped

Optional garnishes: chopped fresh cilantro, crumbled feta and/or seasoned toasted pepitas (not shown)

## INSTRUCTIONS

To roast the spaghetti squash: Preheat the oven to 400 degrees Fahrenheit and line a large baking sheet with parchment paper for easy clean-up. On the baking sheet, drizzle the halved spaghetti squash with olive oil. Rub the olive oil all over each of the halves, adding more if necessary.

Sprinkle the insides of the squash with freshly ground black pepper and salt. Turn them over so the insides are facing down. Roast for 40 to 60 minutes, until the flesh is easily pierced through with a fork.

Meanwhile, to assemble the slaw: In a medium mixing bowl, combine the cabbage, black beans, bell pepper, green onion, cilantro, lime juice, olive oil and salt. Toss to combine and set aside to marinate.

To make the salsa verde: In the bowl of a blender or food processor, combine the avocado, salsa verde, cilantro, lime juice and garlic. Blend until smooth, pausing to scrape down the sides as necessary.

To assemble, first use a fork to separate and fluff up the flesh of the spaghetti squash. Then divide the slaw into each of the spaghetti squash "bowls," and add a big dollop of avocado salsa verde. Finish the bowls with another sprinkle of pepper, cilantro and optional crumbled feta or pepitas.

# KALE AND CAULIFLOWER SOUP

## INGREDIENTS

1 large white or yellow onion, diced (390 g)

4 cloves garlic, minced

3 medium carrots (175 g, approx. 1.5 cups chopped)

1 tsp each dried parsley and ground thyme

1/2 tsp sea salt

6 cups vegetable stock

1 head of cauliflower (775 g, approx. 7 cups chopped)

4 cups lightly packed, chopped, de-stemmed kale (120 g)

salt and pepper, to taste

## INSTRUCTIONS

Saute the onions and garlic in a a few splashes of vegetable stock until they start to soften, about 5 minutes.

Add in the chopped carrots, parsley and thyme. Cook a few more minutes, adding a bit more stock if needed so it doesn't stick.

Add in the vegetable stock and chopped cauliflower.

Simmer until the cauliflower is tender.

Place about 3/4 of the soup into a blender, leaving some pieces of carrot and cauliflower behind so it will be somewhat chunky.

Process until smooth and then pour the blended soup back into the pot.

Turn off the heat and stir in the chopped kale. Let sit for 5-10 minutes before serving to allow kale to soften.


Warm Collard Quinoa Salad

Ingredients

US CUSTOMARY - METRIC

FOR THE QUINOA

1 cup of quinoa

2 cups of water

½ tsp of salt

1 garlic clove — pealed

FOR THE SAUTÉ COLLARD GREENS

1 bunch collard greens

3 garlic cloves — minced

½ onion — diced

1 cup cherry tomatoes

1 tsp extra olive oil

Red pepper flakes — to taste

salt ground black pepper

Instructions

First, place quinoa in a fine strainer. Rinse under cold running water for 2 or 3 minutes and drain for a few minutes.

Bring water to a boil in a medium pan, add the quinoa, a clove of garlic, and salt.

Turn down the heat to medium-low, cover, and cook for about 15 or 20 minutes until the quinoa is fluffy.

Remove the garlic clove from the pan, as it was only used for flavoring.

Cut and trim the stems away from the collard.

Stack a few the leaves on top of each other, roll tightly, and slice.

Wash and set aside to drain.


In a skillet, add the extra virgin olive oil over medium heat.

Add onions, garlic, and red pepper flakes.

Cook until the onions are soft and golden.

Add tomatoes and cook until soft.

Turn the heat to low and add the collard greens, stirring

until wilted.

Finally, add the cooled quinoa and stir well. Season to taste with salt and pepper.

# COCONUT CURRY SOUP W/ SWEET POTATO NOODLES

INGREDIENTS

FOR THE COCONUT CURRY SOUP

1 large sweet potato (spiralized)

1 small white onion (diced)

3 cloves garlic (minced)

1 tablespoon minced fresh ginger

1 red bell pepper (cut into thin strips)

2 tablespoons yellow curry powder, (I used Trader Joe's brand, but use your favorite)

3 cups low-sodium vegetable broth

1 (13.5 ounces) can coconut milk, (I used full fat, but lite would work too)

1/2 cup frozen green peas

Juice of 1/2 lime

## FOR THE GARNISH

Lime wedges

Cilantro

## INSTRUCTIONS

Preheat the oven to 425 degrees F.

Place your spiralized sweet potato noodles on a rimmed baking sheet in one layer (as best as possible). Bake for 10 minutes.

Meanwhile, in a soup pot, sauté the diced onion in 3 tablespoons of water until tender, about 5 to 6 minutes. Add the garlic, ginger, and red bell pepper and sauté 2 minutes more. Add the curry powder, vegetable broth, and coconut milk. Simmer over medium heat for 15 to 20 minutes.

Add the green peas and lime juice and stir to combine.

To serve: ladle individual portions in bowls and then top with sweet potato noodles, lime juice and a sprinkle of chopped cilantro, if desired.

# ONE-POT RED LENTIL AND BUTTERNUT SQUASH CHILI

INGREDIENTS

FOR THE CHILI:

2 tbsp extra virgin olive oil

1 large onion, diced

1 bell pepper, diced

2 jalapeno peppers, de-seeded and diced

2 garlic cloves, minced

2 cups dry red split lentils, rinsed

1.5 lb. (24 oz.) butternut squash, peeled and cut into ½ inch cubes

540 ml (19 fl. oz) canned black beans, drained and rinsed

2½ cups canned crushed tomatoes

1½ cups vegetable broth

## FOR THE CHILI SEASONING:

1 tbsp chili powder

1 tsp ground cumin

1 tsp dried oregano

1 tsp smoked (or sweet) paprika

Salt and pepper, to taste

## OPTIONAL TOPPING IDEAS:

green onions, cheese, sour cream, hot sauce, avocado, tortilla chips

## INSTRUCTIONS

Using a large pot on medium-high heat, add olive oil and saute the onion, bell pepper, and jalapeno, stirring frequently, until the onions are translucent and the peppers begin to soften (about 3-4 minutes).

Then stir in the garlic and chili seasoning, allowing the spices become to become fragrant (about 1-2 minutes).

Add the red lentil, butternut squash, black beans, crushed tomatoes, and vegetable broth and stir until well-combined.

Bring the chili to a boil and then reduce the heat to a simmer. Cover and let it simmer for 25-30 minutes, until the butternut squash and lentils are tender and cooked through. Top with optional ingredients of your choice. Best served warm.

## NOTES

Makes about 12 cups of chili.

Store cooled leftovers in an airtight container for up to 4 days in the refrigerator. Re-heat on the stove-top or microwave.

When keeping for longer than 4 days, place the leftovers in an airtight container or freezer bag (with air-pressed out) and store in the freezer for up to 4 months. Let the frozen chili thaw overnight in the refrigerator before reheating on the stove (add a shallow layer of water to prevent the chili from scorching the pot) or heat it up in the micro-wave.

ONE-POT RED LENTIL AND BUTTERNUT SQUASH CHILI

INGREDIENTS

FOR THE CHILI:

2 tbsp extra virgin olive oil

1 large onion, diced

1 bell pepper, diced

2 jalapeno peppers, de-seeded and diced

2 garlic cloves, minced

2 cups dry red split lentils, rinsed

1.5 lb. (24 oz.) butternut squash, peeled and cut into ½ inch cubes

540 ml (19 fl. oz) canned black beans, drained and rinsed

2½ cups canned crushed tomatoes

1½ cups vegetable broth

FOR THE CHILI SEASONING:

1 tbsp chili powder

1 tsp ground cumin

1 tsp dried oregano

1 tsp smoked (or sweet) paprika

Salt and pepper, to taste

OPTIONAL TOPPING IDEAS:

green onions, cheese, sour cream, hot sauce, avocado, tortilla chips

INSTRUCTIONS

Using a large pot on medium-high heat, add olive oil and saute the onion, bell pepper, and jalapeno, stirring frequently, until the onions are translucent and the peppers begin to soften (about 3-4 minutes).

Then stir in the garlic and chili seasoning, allowing the spices become to become fragrant (about 1-2 minutes).

Add the red lentil, butternut squash, black beans, crushed tomatoes, and vegetable broth and stir until well-combined.

Bring the chili to a boil and then reduce the heat to a simmer. Cover and let it simmer for 25-30 minutes, until the butternut squash and lentils are tender and cooked through. Top with optional ingredients of your choice.

Best served warm.

NOTES

Makes about 12 cups of chili.

Store cooled leftovers in an airtight container for up to 4 days in the refrigerator. Re-heat on the stove-top or microwave.

When keeping for longer than 4 days, place the leftovers in an airtight container or freezer bag (with air-pressed out) and store in the freezer for up to 4 months. Let the frozen chili thaw overnight in the refrigerator before reheating on the stove (add a shallow layer of water to prevent the chili from scorching the pot) or heat it up in the microwave.

METHODHIDE

1 Preheat the oven to 375F. Line a baking sheet with aluminum foil, a silicon baking mat, or parchment paper.

2 Prepare the squash: Cut the squash in half lengthwise. Scoop out and discard the strings and seeds (save and roast the seeds, if you like). Cut the squash into 1-inch slices.

Toss the squash with a 1 tablespoon of olive oil, 1/4 teaspoon or so of salt, and ground black pepper. Place on the prepared baking sheet.

Roasted Winter Squash with Cilantro Chimichurri

3 Roast the squash for 30 minutes or until easily pierced with a fork.

Roasted Winter Squash with Cilantro Chimichurri

4 While the squash is cooking prepare the chimichurri. In a medium bowl, stir together the olive oil, cilantro, parsley, oregano leaves, chili flakes, garlic, red wine vinegar and 1/4 teaspoon salt. Taste and add more salt if needed.

Roasted Winter Squash with Cilantro Chimichurri

5 Serve: Transfer the roasted squash to a serving platter or individual plates, top with a generous amount of chimichurri, and enjoy.

# FRENCH LENTIL & CHICKPEA SOUP (VEGAN)

INGREDIENTS

¼ cup olive oil

1 white onion, chopped

3 garlic cloves, minced or freshly pressed

1 can 15oz tomato sauce (or use pasta sauce)

1 tbsp vegetable base reduced sodium

1 cup french green lentil

5 cups water

1 can 15oz chickpeas, rinsed

1 cup collard greens, thinly sliced (or kale)

Spices

½ tsp red pepper flakes

¼ tsp cumin

¼ tsp curry powder

salt + pepper to taste

INSTRUCTIONS

In a large pot heat the oil, add chopped onion and cook until soft (about 3 mins). Add garlic and cook until fragrant. Add the tomato sauce, stir. Add in spices, vegetable base, water and lentil, stir and cover. Cook for approximately 30 mins then add in the chickpeas.

Take 2 cups of the soup from pot and blend it for 30 secs* if using a Vitamix. Pour the blended soup back in the pot. Add collar greens (or kale) and let it simmer for 5 minutes.

Serve with roasted chickpeas, fresh scallion, toasted sesame seeds or coconut cream.


WARM BUCKWHEAT AND BEETROOT SALAD

INGREDIENTS

2 cups roasted buckwheat (also known as kasha)

3 large beetroots

50 g / 2 oz baby spinach

2-3 large mushrooms (I used portobello ones)

½ leek, white and green part, sliced

2 large garlic cloves, finely diced

1 tsp dried rosemary

1/3 tsp coarse sea salt

black pepper

2 tbsp hazelnuts, chopped

3 tbsp olive oil

1-2 tbsp balsamic vinegar

fresh parsley, to serve

METHOD

Heat up the oven to 200° C / 395° F. Peel beetroots and chop them into a large dice.

In a pestle and mortar, make rosemary salt by pounding dry rosemary and sea salt until you get a fine powder.

Place beetroot chunks in a bowl. Coat in 1 tablespoon of olive oil and 1 tablespoon of balsamic vinegar and season with rosemary salt and pepper. Bake for about 40 minutes, until tender.

Carefully check buckwheat for small stones and debris (I advise against rinsing it though as it becomes mushy). Put buckwheat into a small pot with a glass lid and add 3 cups / 720 ml of water, cover with a lid and bring to the boil. Do not salt it until it's been cooked as salt negatively affects buckwheat's texture. Once the water comes to the boil, turn the heat down to low and cook on a low heat until all the water has been absorbed (to check, tip the pot to see if water is coming out from underneath the buckwheat, but DO NOT LIFT THE LID). Once the water has been fully absorbed, rest the pot for another 10 minutes (with the lid firmly on) so that the buckwheat finishes cooking in its own steam.

Heat up the remaining two tablespoons of olive oil in a pan. Add sliced leeks and fry, on a low heat, until almost soft. Add diced garlic and fry until translucent and fragrant. Add sliced mushrooms and fry until cooked. Season with salt and pepper and a tablespoon of balsamic vinegar. Allow it to cook out. Add spinach and allow it to wilt into the salad. Finally add cooked buckwheat. Mix well and adjust the seasoning.

Divide between bowls, top with roasted beetroot chunks, hazelnuts and some fresh parsley.

Ratatouille

INGREDIENTS

1 cup crushed tomatoes

1 Tablespoon extra virgin olive oil

1/4 teaspoon apple cider vinegar

1 teaspoon minced garlic

1 Tablespoon fresh basil, about 3-4 large leaves, sliced , plus more for garnish

1 teaspoon herbs de Provence spice mix

1/4 teaspoon salt

1/4 teaspoon black pepper

1/4 teaspoon chili powder

1 medium sweet or red onion,, sliced

1-2 large zucchini, (about 1 1/2 cups slices, sliced)

1 large Japanese eggplant, (about 3 cups slices, sliced)

3 large fresh tomatoes, (roma is best; about 3 cups slices, sliced)

INSTRUCTIONS

Preheat oven to 350F. Lightly grease a 6"x9" baking dish and set aside. (see notes for baking in an 8"x8" square pan)

In a medium mixing bowl, combine the crushed tomatoes, oil and vinegar. Stir in the garlic, basil, herbs de Provence, salt, pepper, and chili powder.

Pour the tomato mixture into the prepared baking dish and smooth it into an even layer on the bottom of the pan.

Stack the veggie slices in alternating patters (e.g.: onion, zucchini, eggplant, tomato; repeat) and place them on their side in the pan, leaning against the edge of the pan. Repeat until you've formed a couple of rows of veggies, filled the pan, and used up all of the veggie slices.

Optionally, spray or brush the exposed tops of the veggies with oil to encourage browning in the oven. This is more for appearance, so feel free to skip this step if you want.

Bake for about an hour, until the tomato sauce at the bottom is bubbling and the veggies are tender.

Garnish with additional chopped fresh basil before serving (optional). Serve hot or cold.

# VEGAN CLASSIC LEEK AND POTATO SOUP

Ingredients

2 tbsp olive oil

1 large white onion sliced

10 cloves garlic smashed

3 large leeks trimmed, cleaned, and sliced

3 large potatoes washed and cut into bite-sized chunks

3 L vegetable broth

Freshly ground black pepper and snipped chives to serve

Instructions

Sauté the onion in the oil until it becomes translucent, then add the garlic, and continue to cook for 3-4 minutes, until the raw garlic smell has gone.

Add the leeks and potatoes, and give everything a good stir. Cover the pan, and allow everything to sweat for 10 minutes.

Add the stock, stir again to make sure everything gets mixed together, replace the lid, and raise the heat under the pan to bring the soup to a boil.

As soon as it starts boiling, turn the heat down, and allow the soup to simmer for around 30 minutes, or until all the vegetables are soft.

When it's ready, remove the pan from the heat, and blend everything together, until smooth.

Ladle into bowls, and finish with a grind of black pepper and a few snipped chives.

This potato and leek soup will keep for up to three days in an airtight container in the fridge, or three months in the freezer.

Winter Buddha Bowl

Ingredients

Falafel

1 Recipe Winter Kale Falafel

Roasted Carrots

6 Small Carrots sliced into rounds

Drizzle of Extra Virgin Olive Oil

1/4 Tsp Smoked Paprika

Pinch of Salt and Pepper to taste

Pearl Couscous

1 Cup Pearl Couscous

1/2 Small Red Beet peeled and shredded

1 Tbs Extra Virgin Olive Oil

Juice from 1/2 of a Lemon

1/4 Tsp Salt

1/4 Tsp Pepper

Herby Tahini Sauce

1/3 Cup Tahini

1 Clove Garlic

1/3 Cup Parsley

1/3 Cup Water

Juice from 1/2 Lemon

1/4 Tsp Salt

1/4 Tsp Pepper

The Rest of the Bowl

Kale or Hardy Winter Greens

Pumpkin Seeds

Sesame Seeds

Fresh Cracked Black Pepper

Instructions

Roasted Carrots

Preheat the oven to 400 degrees F.

Wash and slice the carrots into rounds. In a bowl, toss with olive oil, smoked paprika, and salt and pepper.

On a baking sheet, bake carrots for 20 minutes, or until softened.

When done, let cool and set aside.

Pearl Couscous

While carrots are cooking, bring a pot of water to boil. Once water is boiling, add in couscous and cook like you would pasta, for as long as the package indicates.

When done, drain water from couscous and put it back in the pot.

Add in shredded beets, olive oil, lemon juice, salt and pepper, and mix well. Taste and adjust seasonings as needed. Set aside.

Herby Tahini Sauce

In a blender, combine all sauce ingredients. Blend on high until smooth and creamy.

Putting It All Together

Take out two large bowls. Portion out half the couscous and carrots into one bowl, the remaining halves in the other. Add in as much falafel and greens as you like. Top everything with the herby tahini sauce, and garnish with pumpkin seeds and sesame seeds if desired.

Enjoy!

sesame kabocha squash with tahini sauce

1 pound kabocha squash

1 tablespoon sesame oil

1 cup cooked brown rice

2 cups baby spinach

Sesame seeds (for serving)

Red pepper flakes (for serving)

tahini sauce

1/4 cup tahini

1 clove garlic (minced)

1 teaspoon fresh minced ginger

2 teaspoons sesame oil

2 teaspoons low-sodium soy sauce or tamari

Juice from half a lemon

2 tablespoons water

Heat oven to 400° F. Prep the squash by washing, drying, and cutting into ½" thick slices with the skin still on (or if you prefer, remove the skin). Toss the squash with the sesame oil and spread into a single layer on a sheet tray. Roast until the squash is tender and browning, 30 to 40 minutes.

While the squash is roasting, combine the ingredients for

the tahini sauce in a bowl and whisk until well combined.

Assemble the bowls with the rice, spinach, roasted squash, a drizzle of the tahini sauce, and a sprinkle of sesame seeds and red pepper flakes.

Tips & Tricks: Roast the kabocha squash until the skin on the squash is edible. If the squash is older or you're not sure, cut the squash into wedges and remove the skin before roasting.

NOURISHING WINTER RAINBOW SALAD (V+, P, R, GrF, GF, NF)

INGREDIENTS FOR THE SALAD:

4 cups of loosely packed thinly sliced red cabbage (about ¼ of a cabbage)

4 cups of loosely packed thinly sliced kale (about 8-10 leaves, stems removed)

2 cups of loosely packed chopped parsley

½ cup pumpkin seeds and/or crushed almonds

seeds from 1 pomegranate

one sliced green apple (optional)

INGREDIENTS FOR THE DRESSING:

6 tablespoons extra virgin olive oil

4 tablespoons freshly squeezed lime juice (from about 2 limes)

2 tablespoon white almond butter (like this one here)

½-inch piece fresh ginger, grated

½ teaspoon sea salt

1-2 tablespoons of (filtered) water (optional, see tips)


How to make vegan winter rainbow salad - The Little Plantation

INSTRUCTIONS:

Please wash all the ingredients for the salad. Remove the stem of the kale (you can you it in this juice, so please don't throw it away) and also remove the hard core of the cabbage. Then thinly slice the kale, cabbage and parsley and mix together in a large bowl with the pumpkin seeds and/or crushed almonds. Now also add the pomegranate seeds. If you are using the green apple, please cut it in thin slices and add it to the salad too.

In a separate small container mix together the olive oil, lime juice, water, almond butter, grated ginger and salt. Dress the salad just before serving and enjoy!

Tip 1: You can replace the red cabbage with savoy cabbage if need be.

Tip 2: To keep this nut-free, please replace the almond butter with tahini.

Tip 3: If you prefer a slightly sweeter salad, I would suggest using the apple noted in the recipe and replacing the pomegranate seed with dried cranberries or sweet grapes.

Tip 4: You can also add 1-2 cups of grated fennel as it works very well with this salad too.

Tip 5: You can add water to the dressing to make it slightly runnier IF YOU LIKE. This step is optional. I suggest making it without water first, checking for consistency and then adding a tablespoon of water at a time to get it to the consistency yu like.

# EASY SPICY VEGETABLE SOUP

INGREDIENTS

2 T . extra virgin olive oil

1 onion , chopped

2-3 cloves garlic , minced

3 carrots , peeled and chopped

2 stalks of celery , chopped

1 red pepper , chopped

1 medium zucchini , chopped

1 tsp thyme

1-2 T Old Bay seasoning

1 15 oz diced tomatoes

4-5 c vegetable broth/stock

1 c frozen green beans

1 sweet potato (medium size) , peeled and diced

INSTRUCTIONS

Heat oil in a large soup pot.

Add onions and sweat for 4-5 minutes.

Add garlic and cook for 1-2 minutes.

Add carrots and celery and cook for 3-5 minutes.

Add pepper and zucchini and cook for 3-5 minutes.

Add thyme and Old Bay and cook for 1-2 minutes.

Add remaining ingredients and cook until starting to simmer.

Turn down heat to low, cover soup, and cook until sweet potatoes are cooked for approximately 15 minutes.


## STUFFED ZA'ATAR ROASTED ACORN SQUASH W/ PEPPER-LEMON TAHINI SAUCE

INGREDIENTS

3 acorn squash, washed and cut in half

2 tablespoons za'atar

2 cups chickpeas, cooked (or a 15oz can of chickpeas, drained and rinsed)

1 medium shallot, diced

3 large kale leaves, destemmed and shredded

1/2 tablespoon extra virgin olive oil

1 teaspoon ground cumin

1/8 teaspoon cayenne (optional)

1/2 cup quinoa, cooked

salt + pepper

sesame seeds, for garnish

pepper-lemon tahini sauce

1/4 cup tahini paste

1 tablespoon fresh lemon juice

1/4 teaspoon freshly ground pepper

1 clove garlic, minced

sea salt

INSTRUCTIONS

preheat oven to 400° and line a rimmed baking sheet with parchment. place squash cut side up, and brush with olive oil; season with a pinch of salt for each, and evenly sprinkle the za'atar spice. place in oven and bake until fork-tender; roughly 40-50 minutes. remove from oven and set aside

while squash are cooking, heat a 8-10 inch skillet on medium, once hot, add the olive oil and shallot; saute shallot for a few minutes, until translucent and soft. add the chickpeas, cumin, and cayenne pepper, and a couple pinches of salt; cook for 1 to 2 minutes. add the kale and cook until a bit wilted, 1 to 2 minutes. remove from heat and set aside in a large mixing bowl, combine the sauteed chickpeas and kale, with the quinoa.  taste for seasoning and adjust if needed

stuff each squash half with roughly a 1/2 cup quinoa mix (more or less depending on the size of your acorn squash). serve warm with a few drizzles of the tahini sauce, and sesame seeds

Vegetable Wild Rice Soup

INGREDIENTS

1 medium onion, finely chopped

2 medium carrots, sliced

1/2 bell pepper, chopped

2 cloves garlic, minced (1 teaspoon)

8 ounces mushrooms, sliced

2 cups green beans (fresh or frozen)

2 teaspoons dried basil

1 teaspoon dried oregano

1/2 teaspoon smoked paprika

1 15-ounce can diced tomatoes

1 32-ounce (4 cups) container vegetable broth

2 cups water

1 cup wild rice

1 15-ounce can white beans, drained and rinsed

3/4 cup organic corn kernels (canned or frozen)

2 cups spinach, chopped

Salt and pepper, to taste

INSTRUCTIONS

In a large pot, heat a little water or oil over medium heat.

Add onion; cook for 5-7 minutes, until they begin to brown. Add carrots and bell pepper; cook for 3 minutes. Add garlic; cook for 1 minute.

Add mushrooms, green beans, basil, oregano, and smoked paprika. Stir until the vegetables are evenly coated in spices; cook for 3-4 minutes.

Add diced tomatoes, broth, water and wild rice. Bring to a boil. Cover, reduce heat to simmer, and cook for 45 minutes.

Add beans, corn, and spinach. Cook until the spinach is wilted. Serve hot.

# WARM QUINOA AND ROASTED VEGETABLE SALAD

Ingredients

The Quinoa

1 cup quinoa

1 & ¼ cups water

¼ teaspoon salt

The Veggies

about 1 pound of butternut squash, cut into 1 & ½ inch cubes

14 ounces of fresh Brussels sprouts, trimmed and cut in half, from top to bottom

1 large, or up to 4 small red onions, peeled and cut into chunks about the same size as the squash.

A few sprigs of fresh thyme, or ½ teaspoon dried thyme, sprinkled over the veggies

olive oil

kosher salt & fresh ground black pepper

The Vinaigrette

Juice of 1 lemon

1 minced clove of garlic

1 teaspoon Dijon mustard

pinch of sugar

½ teaspoon kosher salt

7-8 grinds black pepper

⅓ cup of good quality olive oil

Instructions

Cook the Quinoa

Rinse the quinoa well, and drain in a fine mesh strainer.

Using a medium saucepan, combine the rinsed quinoa with the water and salt.

Bring to a simmer and cook, with the lid left open a crack, for about 15 minutes, until most of the water is absorbed - it may take a little longer, so just give it a few more minutes if you need to.

When the quinoa is done, leave the lid on and set aside.

Roast the Veggies

While the quinoa is cooking, place all of the vegetables on a large baking sheet, and drizzle generously with olive oil. Stir around to get it all evenly coated, and sprinkle with the salt and pepper. Break the thyme stems into smaller pieces, and scatter among the vegetables.

Roast in a 400º oven for about 30 minutes, stirring a couple times, until everything is cooked nicely, and can be pierced with the tip of a pairing knife fairly easily.

Make the Vinaigrette

In a small bowl, whisk the lemon juice with the garlic, mustard, sugar, salt and pepper, until the salt and sugar are dissolved.

Whisk in the oil, in a thin stream to combine and emulsify the vinaigrette

Assemble the Dish

When the veggies are tender and cooked through, take a nice serving bowl and layer the cooked quinoa in the bottom. Put about half of the veggies on top, making sure to remove the stems from the thyme, and gently combine the veg and and quinoa. Kind of mound it in the center a bit, and then scatter the remaining vegetables over the top. Drizzle with a couple tablespoons of the vinaigrette.

Serve warm, and store leftovers in the fridge.

# CARROT, RED LENTIL, & SPINACH SOUP

Ingredients

1 teaspoon olive oil

1/2 red onion, chopped

5-6 medium carrots, about 3 cups, cut into 1cm (3/4 in.) slices

3 cloves garlic, minced

3 cm piece fresh ginger, minced

1/2 teaspoon cumin

1/2 teaspoon turmeric

1/2 teaspoon fresh ground pepper

1/4 teaspoon cayenne pepper (to taste)

1 teaspoon sea salt (to taste)

400 grams (13.5 oz.) canned diced tomatoes

1.5 litres (6 cups) vegetable stock

150 grams (1 cup) red lentils

150 grams (1 cup) frozen spinach**

Juice of 1/2 a lemon

Brown rice, to serve

Instructions

In a large pot, heat the oil over medium. Add the onion and sauté for a couple of minutes or until soft and fragrant. Stir in the carrots, and cook for another minute or two.

Add the garlic, ginger, and spices, stirring to coat the vegetables. Now add the salt and tomatoes, stir, and pour the vegetable stock in.

Increase the heat to high, cover the pot, and bring the soup to a rolling boil. Add the lentils and reduce the heat to medium-low and simmer for 20-25 minutes, covered, or until the carrots are tender.

Stir in the spinach and turn off the heat, letting the hot soup thaw the spinach with the lid on. Add the lemon juice, taste, and season with salt if necessary.

Serve over brown rice and store leftovers in the refrigerator or freezer.

Vegan Sweet Potato Soup with Spicy Chickpea Croutons

Ingredients

For the Chickpea Croutons:

2 cans each 15.5 ounces of cooked garbanzo beans (aka chickpeas), drained and rinsed

2 tablespoons olive oil

1/2 teaspoon garlic powder

1/2 teaspoon ground cumin

1/4 teaspoon ground cinnamon

1/2 teaspoon salt

1/2 teaspoon ground black pepper

For The Sweet Potato Soup:

1 tablespoon vegetable oil

1/2 teaspoon ground coriander

1 teaspoon ground cumin

2 medium-sized onions chopped

2 cloves of garlic minced

1 teaspoon of grated ginger from 1 inch fresh ginger

1 teaspoon kosher salt

1/2 teaspoon black pepper

2 medium-sized Sweet Potatoes peeled and cut into small cubes (appr. 5-6 cups)

2 carrots peeled and sliced (appr. 1 cup)

6 cups vegetable stock

1/4 cup fresh cilantro or parsley for garnish chopped

Instructions

Start with roasting the chickpea croutons:

Preheat the oven to 400 degrees. Line a baking sheet with parchment paper. Set aside.

Lay two layers of paper towels on a kitchen counter. Spread the rinsed garbanzo beans (chickpeas) to dry. With the help of another piece of paper towel, dry the beans as much as possible. Once dried, transfer them to a mixing bowl.

Mix the oil, spices, and hot sauce (if using) in a small bowl. Drizzle it over the chickpeas, making sure that they are coated with the oil and spice mixture.

Spread the chickpeas on the baking sheet and bake for 20-25 minutes, until crisp and golden, tossing a couple of times during the baking to ensure even cooking.

Take them out of the oven and set aside to cool.

To make the soup:

Heat the oil in a Dutch oven (or any other heavy bottom pan) in medium heat. Add in the ground cumin and coriander. Add the onion. Cook, stirring occasionally, over medium heat, until translucent, 7-8 minutes.

Stir in the garlic and ginger, salt and pepper, and sautee, stirring constantly, for 45 seconds.

Stir in the sweet potatoes and carrot and mix until coated with the spices and onions, 1-2 minutes.

Pour in the vegetable stock and bring it to a boil. Once boiled, turn down the heat to low and let it simmer for 20 minutes or until sweet potatoes are soft.

Puree the soup in a blender or a food processor in batches. Return it back to the pot and heat until warm.

If you feel that it is too thick, you can add in a little bit of water and bring it to a boil.

When ready to serve, garnish the soup with a handful of chickpea croutons and fresh herbs.

# ROASTED BUTTERNUT SQUASH, KALE AND CRANBERRY COUSCOUS

INGREDIENTS

COUSCOUS SALAD INGREDIENTS:

1 small butternut squash, peeled, seeded, and diced into 1/2-inch cubes

2 tablespoons olive oil

salt and freshly-cracked black pepper

1 cup dry Israeli (pearl) couscous*, cooked in water according to package instructions

2 cups chopped kale leaves

1/3 cup dried cranberries (from DeLallo Salad Savors)

1/3 cup chopped walnuts (from DeLallo Salad Savors)

2 ounces goat cheese, crumbled (from DeLallo Salad Savors)

easy orange vinaigrette (recipe below)

VINAIGRETTE INGREDIENTS:

2 tablespoons apple cider vinegar

2 tablespoons DeLallo extra virgin olive oil

2 tablespoons freshly-squeezed orange juice

pinch of salt and black pepper, to taste

INSTRUCTIONS

TO MAKE THE COUSCOUS SALAD:

Heat oven to 425°F.

In a large mixing bowl, toss cubed butternut squash with olive oil. Sprinkle with a few generous pinches of salt and pepper, and toss until combined.

Spread the butternut squash out in an even layer on a parchment-covered baking sheet. Bake for 15 minutes, then remove from the oven and flip the squash for even cooking. Bake for an additional 10-15 minutes, or until the squash is tender and slightly browned around the edges. Remove from oven and transfer back to the large mixing bowl.

Add couscous, kale, cranberries, walnuts, goat cheese, and vinaigrette, and toss to combine.

Serve warm, or refrigerate in a sealed container for up to 3 days.

## TO MAKE THE VINAGIRETTE:

Whisk all ingredients together until combined. Taste, and season with additional salt and pepper if needed.

Winter Veggie Power Bowl

Ingredients

Veggie Power Bowl

2 tablespoons avocado oil (divided)

3 cups cubed butternut squash (415 grams)

3 medium parsnips, peeled and cubed (2 heaping cups/270 grams)

1 teaspoon garlic powder

1 large beet, peeled and cubed (2 cups/275 grams)

1/2 teaspoon cumin

6 cups packed kale, roughly chopped (180 grams)

1/3 cup walnuts (roughly chopped)

1/3 cup dried cranberries

1 small small avocado, sliced (100 grams)

salt and pepper, to taste

additional add ons: quinoa, chickpeas, roasted chicken, goat cheese...

## Vegan Tahini Dressing

2 tablespoons tahini

2 tablespoons coconut aminos

1 tablespoon lemon juice

1 teaspoon apple cider vinegar

1/4 teaspoon ground ginger

1/4 teaspoon garlic powder

1/4-1/2 teaspoon red pepper flakes

salt and pepper, to taste

Instructions

Preheat oven to 375 degrees Fahrenheit. Line 1-2 large baking sheets with parchment paper.

Roast the veggies. In a medium bowl mix together butternut squash, parnships, 1 tablespoon avocado oil, garlic powder, and salt and pepper. Place on baking sheet making sure veggies are spread out evenly. In the same bowl add beets, 1/2 tablespoon avocado oil, cumin, and salt and pepper and mix to combine. Place on same baking sheet or another one if more room is needed. Roast for 35-40 minutes until soft and fork tender

While the vegetables roast, place kale in a bowl and massage with 1/2 tablepsoon avocado oil and a pinch of salt and pepper until leaves become tender and soft.

Make the dressing. Mix all ingredients into a bowl and

whisk to combine. Add a little water if you want a thinner consistency or more tahini if you want it thicker.

When veggies are done assemble the bowls. Divide kale, roasted veggies, walnuts, cranberries, and avocado between 3 bowls. Top with dressing and enjoy!

# CREAMY VEGAN BUTTERNUT SQUASH SOUP WITH ROASTED VEGETABLES

INGREDIENTS

Soup

1 butternut squash, halved and seeds removed

1 acorn squash, halved and seeds removed

olive oil

2 Tablespoons olive oil

1/2 cup vegetable stock

1–2 cans of full-fat coconut milk

pinch of salt

optional: 1 Teaspoon ground cinnamon

Sauteed Vegetables:

2 cups broccoli florets

4 large carrots, diced

2 cups mushrooms, sliced

2 Tablespoons olive oil

salt

INSTRUCTIONS

Soup

Preheat oven to 400 degrees.

Lay butternut squash and acorn squash, inner sides up, on deep cookie sheet.

Take olive oil and ensure each piece is lightly coated all over.

Pour water in bottom of pan, just enough to cover the bottom.

Bake for 1 hour.

Scoop out squash and place in dutch oven.

Pour in vegetable stock and 1 can of coconut milk.

Use immersion blender to fully combine.

Add pinch of salt and stir.

Taste and add any cinnamon you desire.

Additionally, if you want it even creamier, add the second can of coconut milk and use the immersion blender to combine.

If you need to make it sweeter, feel free to had a couple splashes of real maple syrup.

Sauteed Vegetables:

While soup is keeping warm on the stove, combine vegetables in medium bowl and drizzle with olive oil and sprinkle with salt.

Roast at 425 on a foil-lined baking sheet for 10-15 minutes, tossing halfway.

Serve soup with a side of vegetables for people to add as they choose.

Feel free to garnish with basil leaves and bean sprouts, if desired

# CONCLUSION

his chapter reviewed the multiple studies on growth and development of children and adolescents on various vegetarian diets. Case studies of malnutrition in children on various alternative diets have not been discussed, because it is evident that these are incidental and do not necessarily represent ubiquitous nutritional deficiencies in these various types of vegetarian populations.

To ensure a practical approach based on type of diet, the multiple investigations on vegetarian children have been assembled in three groups of studies

SDA vegetarian children are generally lacto-ovo-vegetarians or lacto-vegetarians and the results of these studies show no marked differences in physical growth and development when compared with standard references or with non-vegetarian SDA children. We can therefore conclude that a lacto-(ovo)-vegetarian diet generally results in normal growth.

, the patterns of animal food avoidance in vegetarians may vary considerably from group to group. This is true within a particular category of vegetarians, such as lacto-ovo-vegetarians, as well as between the different types. A pure vegetarian or vegan diet does not seem to preclude optimal growth and development, provided a well-planned and balanced plant-based diet is followed with appropriate supplements of fortified foods. Even with careful balance, both the parents and the physician should be aware that growth might be slower than expected. This, however, does not mean that this slow growth can be equated per se with poor health.


A macrobiotic diet is far more restrictive than a lacto-ovo-vegetarian, or even a vegan diet, particularly when the most desirable degree of macrobiotic regimen is followed. The most severe cases of malnutrition among infants following unconventional dietary practices seem to have been associated with macrobiotics.14 The macrobiotic studies cited in the present review confirm potential nutritional problems with regard to growth and development of infants and children fed on a macrobiotic diet. It seems unlikely, in contrast to vegetarianism, that children raised on a higher level of macrobiotic regimen can thrive well.